THIS MORNING IS DIFFERENT

poems by

Mistee St. Clair

Finishing Line Press
Georgetown, Kentucky

THIS MORNING IS DIFFERENT

Copyright © 2021 by Mistee St. Clair
ISBN 978-1-64662-575-8 First Edition
All rights reserved under International and Pan-American Copyright Conventions. No part of this book may be reproduced in any manner whatsoever without written permission from the publisher, except in the case of brief quotations embodied in critical articles and reviews.

ACKNOWLEDGMENTS

Grateful acknowledgements to the following publications in which these poems first appeared.

Anchorage Daily News: "Bloom"
Cirque Journal: "Until Then" and "Gray" (previously published as "Gris")
Sky Island Journal: "After He Died, She Returned out of Habit," "Sunflowers Bloom in December" and "Picking Crabapples"
Tidal Echoes: "Notes to My Husband, the Sailor," and "Lately, Walking the Dog"

I would like to thank my dear friend Patty Ware for all her thoughtful comments, suggestions, and for being there; the Burn Thompson Writers Group for their quick wit; Cathleen, whom I have known since I was two and, even though we haven't lived in the same place since we were seven, has remained my best friend and is always ready to talk writing; and my patient, supportive, hilarious family for reminding me, again and again, to embrace the rain.

Publisher: Leah Huete de Maines
Editor: Christen Kincaid
Cover Art: Lora Brown
Author Photo: Jon St. Clair
Cover Design: Elizabeth Maines McCleavy

Order online: www.finishinglinepress.com
also available on amazon.com

Author inquiries and mail orders:
Finishing Line Press
PO Box 1626
Georgetown, Kentucky 40324
USA

Table of Contents

Until Then 1

Home 2

Bloom 3

Gray 4

Caught 5

Notes to my Husband, the Sailor 7

Sunflowers Bloom in December 9

After He Died, She Returned Out of Habit 10

Wolves in March 11

Lately, Walking the Dog 12

Picking Crabapples 13

Nights Like These 15

The Room 16

You Want to Talk 17

Penumbral Eclipse 18

My Son and I Fight 19

When Crocuses Bloom 20

Faith 22

This Morning Is Different 23

Until Then

Until the world's beauty becomes enough, I will write about it.
I will write about how some mornings are so dark
the sky is an old brown bruise telling stories of longing:
the dawn for the day, the day for the night, the night for the dawn.
I will write about how some mornings I am mouthed by fog,
a blanket of the cold thick breath of day, and I cannot see beyond.
And how on those days the mountains are terrible, gatekeepers of light.
Until then, I will break apart each ray of sun
as I break apart each poem.
Because some mornings I wait by the window,
looking out toward the channel,
and there is enough light to name a painting hope. Maybe then.
But there is always want. I will tell of it.

Home

If I could say everything I wanted to say
it would be that the hollow crush of snow
and black nights are lonely, but spring
rubs downy willow catkins against the cheek.
I should've held to the willow, which holds
strong but bends well to thick layers of snow
and fast currents on the banks of rivers.
Rivers are roads and carve marks in the land.
Until I left my landmarks I didn't know
I wove my whole being to place
so that its maps were my memories.
Memories are fickle and I fear I will forget
names, thick like chocolate in my mouth:
Chena, Yukon, Fishcamp: Home
exists both in body and earth.
Earth is a river the current of my heart,
the land maps my body with mountains and valleys.
I am a valley of gold, hills of gold dust,
rust gold rivers. A fleck of gold weighs more
than the sun and the heart's heavy sighing.

Bloom

You may leave but it will never leave you,
some body of water. Where the winds
are a second skin that smell of smoky campfires
and salted fish, clean and inviting.
Where fish are practical, whales are cousins,
and boats are objects of beauty
to be admired like architecture.
If the winds had colors, they'd be fat ribbons
that let loose or tie depending on the mood of the water,
which is so deep it is as blurred as the sky.
But the mountains envelop this water, and cradle any sun
that pigments their curvy sides.
This is where your children sing and run naked in their boots,
their eyes shining and cheeks lacing pink.
You run too, the fish run,
fireweed pink as roe bloom, bloom as you.

Gray

Here nothing snarls but trees,
the sky white gray and lucid,
water flowing in all forms.
The land absent of what is missed most,
only old homes and moss hanging
off the graying bark of apple trees.
The hills don't hide the world beyond,
but the fog does. What here, I wonder,
could fill the womb of home, familiarity,
a sense of place? What could stand for
        mountains and trees
        thick with snow and ice,
        the world a white yawn
        that shimmers like teeth;
        homes of plywood splintered
        paint the color of fireweed;
        dogs singing in the long dark;
        the dawn so fresh and confident
        that I may look out the window and say
        "Today I will climb that mountain."
But instead I say "Today I will write a poem."
And I am here, in this place
of gray and green as many shades
as names for snow. Here, I say,
knock mud from your boots,
come have tea from rain, listen, listen,
my body thunders with longing.
Brush against me and I will quake.

Caught

Some mornings, I wake still dreaming
I am a songbird caught

in a research net at Creamer's Field,
where in the winter

the sun is stainless and fog hangs
like a sheet of ice over the fields.

Spring through fall, the voices
of geese, sandpipers, sandhill cranes

gurgle from the grasses and wetlands
and in the boreal forest,

the chatter of squirrels
and dozens of bird songs.

Years ago, I brought the boys to my favorite spots,
wandering through the birch in the drifting,

curious way of young children.
Off trail we found a net,

and this is where my memory blurs.
Was there a bird in the net?

Was there an ornithologist skillfully
disentangling the bird, did we ask questions?

Was it even really a net for songbirds,
or for flying squirrels or little brown bats?

Or was this a dream, a longing for home
I had merged into belief? What I do remember

is imagining ourselves as ornithologists,
holding small lives in our palms,

tiny hearts beating against our loose grip;
we imagined ourselves as the caught birds,

limbs, leaves and trees a blur
until a sudden stillness as we hit the net;

we imagined what it would be like
to be held by those nimble hands,

our halluces plucked from the webbing,
to be set free only to return, again and again,

called by home, guided by the sun,
the stars, and a magnetic, familiar pulse.

Notes to my Husband, the Sailor

The Early Years
Sometimes, at night, there is no depth
to me, and you find where I begin
and where I end easily. Sometimes
I am bottomless, and you find
no end at all. I roll into you
at night, which is the way
I say I love you.

Mornings you are home, we wake
to children in our bed or spread
out on the floor on blankets
around us. You open the curtains.
Outside, the trees grow
sideways as if winds shape
their yearnings. Out the kitchen window
in the early dawn light, the apple tree
is like a graphite drawing, scraggly
lines etched next to the straight, neat lines
of the chicken coop.

As the sun rises it occurs to me
that the sun doesn't rise at all,
but is still and breathing.

The Middle Years
I must hold on to what assurances
I have here: rivers will never run dry,
there is a long wait after the fireweed fluffs,
and you will come home
to put your hands on my back, sharpen
the knives, make our bed.
That is how you tell me you love me.

At the beach, our boys turn their backs
to the water. One asks why all songs are about love
and I wonder if I said the right thing:
that love is lonely, that songs are art
and art is about loneliness
in some way. Think of how a brush
caresses a landscape.

Our sons are like spiders,
all arms and legs these days.
They come and go like the snow,
like you. It is rare now to wake
with the boys in our bed, wedged
between one son and the dog,
another at the bottom by my feet.

Sometimes I need you to come home.
Loneliness is a pressed flower, slight
yet vibrant between the mountains.
Our sons are the mountains, you are the flower
pressed to me.

Sunflowers Bloom in December

When the sunflowers bloom in December,
pomegranates split and hang from branches like stars.
The season is late, the figs have dried and fallen to dirt.
My grandmother now lives here like she belongs,
her face darkened and ripe.

My grandmother lives here as if she belongs,
a bougainvillea in full bloom.
Her broad fingers point,
her voice speaking the language of the land
in the naming of things,
the words familiar and haunting,
swelling with adoration:
javelina, ocotillo, kumquat,
pinacate. She may say one word—
but mean many.
Like when we say "die," we mean
let me lie under this sun and ask for entrance.

When the day goes dark,
I understand, grandmother, this is the place.
The stars explode in the body and still.
In the desert, everything dies.
Eventually, we find their black shells
and remember life's brilliance.
We pocket the shells and say their names.

After He Died, She Returned Out of Habit

In her winter house she dawdles and paces,
percolating coffee in an old pot speckled like his hair.
She leaves the pot on the stove all day,
turned low and half off the burner.
She wears jeans and his flannel shirts,
puts her hair in curlers.
She cooks meals too large for us, eats little herself.
Her hotcakes, soured until chewy and tart,
are still best with only a dab of butter.

We drink cheap wine and cheap beer,
talk politics, construction projects, life in revision.
She is thin but not birdlike, stout as a cactus.
We wake before dawn to the coyotes
and stretch out on couches, silent,
the coyotes saying all we would care to say.
She is alone in this desert,
where everything grows singular,
and untouched.
I want to stay with her and take care of her,
but she will never need taking care of.

When the cacti flower, she goes north.
She says she will die at home,
in her cabin by herself.
When she can't leave it,
she wouldn't want to.

Wolves in March
> *North Douglas*

It was March, still winter. By dark,
it was fierce as January, and the fire
on the beach bristled with power.
We tidepooled with flashlights on our phones,
the anemones white in the bright light.
A friend showed me an app for stargazing,
we held our phones to the sky and found
the orange dot of Mars. After we were too cold,
so cold our fingers curled, we took the short trail back.
Some of the kids had lingered, so we waited,
our breath hanging between us like wan nebulas.
And then, wolves began to howl. One at first,
then others, and each of us stilled. Not a swish
of jacket, not a crunch of boot. For a long time,
they sang. It was so dark, so black, and the stars
were as blank as a newborn. The wolves sang
and it was like the earth was just born, and space
was just born, and they were singing the stars
out into their places, each chorus pushing a star
farther out and by the end, everything settled.
The night, the darkness, us meager humans,
even the children, we settled
like we'd been rocked and lulled
in a womb we'll never quite remember
and never quite forget.

Lately, Walking the Dog

The wind has been pushing into the front door,
but still, early each morning the dog and I persevere
out of ritual and routine, and my need
to gather the day before it begins.
Beside us, the mountains are gray, penciled in thoughts
and the spruce are black in the shadows of street lights.
Each day now collapses into the previous,
indistinct, lonely and dark.

As we climb the hills, the wind hits the town below
like the sudden shutter of a closet door. The dog
looks almost happy, as if she were a sled dog pushing
into a harness, so happy to work so hard, her snout
extended, her scruffy fur sleeked back,
ears pressed sideways, eyes squinting.
I, too, lean in to the wind,
dragging boots and discontent and absurd layers,
wondering what the hell I am doing here
in this place. Yet here I am, somehow always

softening. As I head for home, the light rises woolen
as the chickadees awaken, chattering and gathering
like neighbors in summer, their joy unwavering,
their voices rising ribbons in this drumming wind.

Picking Crabapples

There was a day last September,
still warm and sunny,
when I walked the beach barefoot
and felt the sun romance my shoulders.
Later, my son and I climbed
our apple tree to pick the wild crabapples
and snack on the thumb-sized fruits.
Last year a bear broke off a bough,
but the tree is middle-aged and sturdy enough
to carry on with a large scar and a new shape.
My son dared me to climb higher.
I had one foot braced against the trunk
and the other in a crook,
my legs split and stretched
as I reached higher and further.
Just a few months before, the little nubs
were small, white blooms.
Then they were ripening,
flushed red-orange like rosehips.
It was too early, we knew,
for the little extra nectar maturity provides,
for the flaming red a good frost would bring.
But I was tempted by his playfulness,
and he by the sun.
When we couldn't reach any higher,
we left the rest for the porcupines.
I didn't know it then,
but those were his last days of youth.
I did not know that he'd cut his hair
and I would feel the lost weight
like a pressed bruise.
I did not know that the next summer
I'd climb the tree only once,

lonely and not so high,
that the apples from then on
would fall to the ground as
bright red globes in October.
I did not know any of this as we lowered
ourselves to the still green earth,
a bittersweet tartness drying my mouth.

Nights Like These

When I wake in the middle of the night
on nights like these,
why not make coffee early,
give in to my day already starting?
How often do I leave the lights off
and listen for the water to boil,
sit still and wait for the coffee to bloom?
The house is motionless on its foundation,
while outside the trees shake and sway
as the gods tumble the globe.
Leaves fly off their benefactors
like scarves torn from slender necks.
The dampened orange
from the street lamps light up the rain
streaking down the windows.
How often do I drink coffee like wine,
filling my mouth with darkness?
It used to be, nights like these,
I was used up with babies,
and all their little worries.
Now there is a future to fill-
we talk of Europe, a boat,
all the places in the world to go.
But I wonder if there is enough of an us
to fill plans. Will all days work towards
nights like these-
waking to a constant storm
brewing beyond the thin walls of carelessness?

The Room

He emerges from his room to keep company
like an acquaintance whose talk is small
and insignificant, and before he closes the door
you get a brief glimpse of a tangle of laundry,
paper, candy wrappers-
and a smell like black banana peels
and smoldering socks looms-

and you think about how the room
knows him best now,
what he shows only himself,
keeps his confidences, his secrets,
everything you no longer know-and then
a sliver of darkness from the crack
as the door slides on its hinge,
the lockset moving towards its strike plate,
and you realize that no matter the hell in there,
you want in.

You Want to Talk

Last night the rain and wind
were at their worst, even the dog
wouldn't go out. I woke again and again
to bushes slapping the house, trees swaying
and dropping flimsy limbs, rain hard pellets
hitting the roof. You slept heavy beside me,
and I couldn't endure the rumble of your snore.
I moved to the hard wood floor of the living room,
where the open curtains let in more of the storm.

The morning claims innocence. You talk
light politics, the kids, even a vague plan
for the future. Out the front window,
the old shore pine is thinner. The buoy swing
has been flung into a branch, the crabapples
shaken to the earth. You want to talk,
but I need to be angry and it is easier
to be angry with the storm, to turn away
from life-altering thoughts;
the weather is safer.

Penumbral Eclipse
Juneau, Alaska

The moon is wild this morning.
I mean big-faced and smiling dopily.
I want to trade places with the dog
who trots beside me with infallible joy;
or learn how to swear in a new language,
just for the sake of something new.
The moon glows like a wishing lantern,
floating still and shining
her white happy light
over this blue winter.
The stars are not fierce,
but just to see them above the mountains,
scattered across our solar system
like hot burning candles,
is something.
Tomorrow morning there will be
a penumbral eclipse:
The more diffuse outer shadow of Earth
falls on the moon's face. There is never
a dark bite taken out of the moon,
it never reaches dramatic minutes of totality.
I want to see it, this slight shading
that most won't notice.
It is not a spectacular event,
it is not rare. But I want to know
if I step outside at 8:07am,
will this bald joy be any more, or less?
The forecast says tomorrow will bring
a cold, gray veil of clouds. The usual cloak.
But I will face the shifting sky-
and if I have to, imagine our earth
slipping a shade over the moon's lamp,
as if to smother her mad energy
like something that has lost its everything.

My Son and I Fight
after "Cold" by Ellen Bass

On this early fall morning,
my son and I fight before breakfast,
before school, before the day
has the opportunity to be good.
Of course, I immediately want to give up
and yield to his approaching adulthood.
I want to tell him I might be wrong.
But after fifteen minutes, I cannot let go,
and he goes silent. For a moment
I remember nursing him so long ago,
my hands broad across his bare back
and pressing him to my breasts with a sudden,
wild love of his smell, his folds, his velvety neck-
it seems possible that those insatiable minutes
were preemptive appeals for forgiveness
for days like these when my hands are cold
and my grip tight, for days like these
when I would fail.

When Crocuses Bloom

Winter starts in fall,
when the forget-me-nots stand
small but firm under frost.

In the closing dark, we are
still friends. Eventually, snow
blankets, then turns to ice

and hardens. I sleep
on a roll up mattress on the floor
in front of the fire. My body

aches in the morning, but I rise
from the cold hard wood rested.
I still make your coffee. Alone,

I study our hearts. Blood makes
two circuits, away and towards.
The first and second heart sounds

thumping as valves snap
shut. There is no going back.
I think about how blood flows

more freely when expectation
loses its grip. I learn how to love
you without touching, without

asking. One day it snows, the next,
rain. Winter is a season. We have made
a home, let's lie in it, let's warm ourselves

in its shelter, struggle side by side,
for one more turn. When the snow withdraws,
crocuses will bloom. When the crocuses

bloom, you will ask me
to vacate your heart. I will say
I already have. I will. I'm trying.

Faith

By the time the first snow reached sea level,
I had put the extra wool blanket on the bed

for my cold toes. The floor got old or maybe
I needed your hand on my hip

at night. We've survived another year
in a northern rainforest. Sometime

in the night you throw the blankets
onto me. The heat under the wool rouses

me and I lie awake listening
to the too early morning. Summer

was hard, the world complicated
between us. It rained a lot. I wonder

if this will be a snow heavy year,
if I will worry about avalanches.

The mountains seem fat already. Still,
I move through our glacial terrain

with some kind of faith, choosing
the long view, somehow knowing

it'll be ok, knowing winter
serves spring. It's the only way

to keep going. What we have is good
footing, enough anchors to hold.

This Morning Is Different

There have been no birds
in the yard this morning-
I have nothing to do these days
but observe them.
I'd like the visit of the common robin
sitting on the fence
with her wings slightly drooped,
her intent study of the grass
matching my study of her.
A small flock of starlings could land,
skitter across the yard like marbles,
then fly off abrupt as a streetlight
going out at midnight.
This morning is different.
The leaves of the rhodies are unfurling,
laying up like a sunbather lays out,
glossy under the spring sun.
Where is the song sparrow?
Watching him is my new morning habit.
I miss his little body beyond the window
in the unleafed cherry tree,
hunkered down, puffed up,
an old man in his fat coat,
his little beak raised up,
singing, singing-
I had thought his song was desperate,
a prayer. But now I see,
I am the beggar here.

Mistee St. Clair was born in the interior of Alaska. Of Tanana Athabascan descent and an enrolled member of the Native Village of Minto, she has spent most of her life in Alaska. The natural world and the weather influence her writing. Currently she lives in Juneau, a temperate rainforest, where she raises two sons and works seasonally for the Alaska State Legislature.

www.ingramcontent.com/pod-product-compliance
Lightning Source LLC
LaVergne TN
LVHW040118080426
835507LV00041B/1768